# The Shrimp

By: Laura Nicholas

# The shrimp swims.

# The shrimp jumps.

# The shrimp splashes.

# The shrimp swims past a shell.

# The shrimp swims past a fish.

The shrimp spots a big fish.
The shrimp dashes past a rock.
The big fish did not get the shrimp.

# The shrimp swims.
# The shrimp is glad.

# The Chest

By: Laura Nicholas

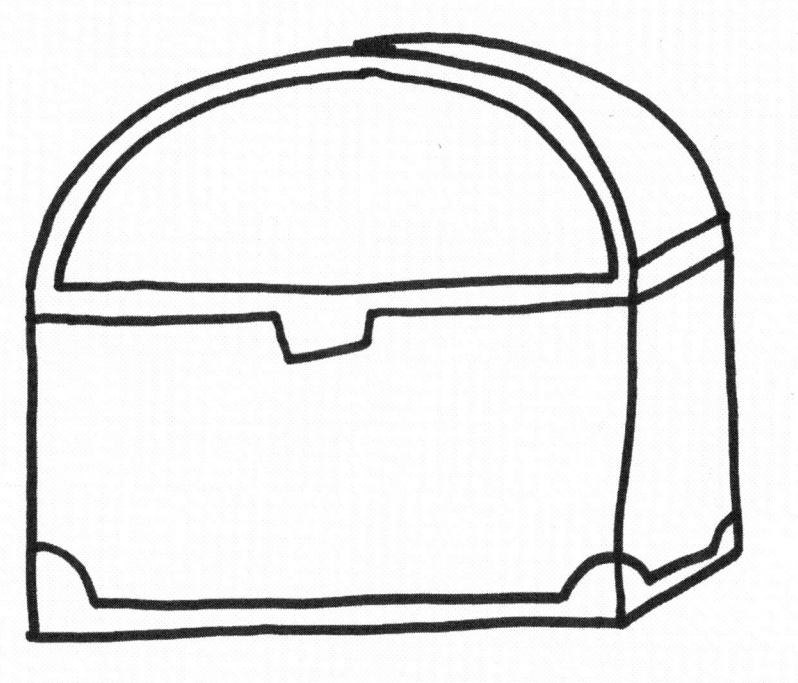

A bench is on the grass.
Pat sits on the bench.

# Max has a chest.
# Max sets the chest on the bench.

# Is a chick in the chest?
# Is a chimp in the chest?

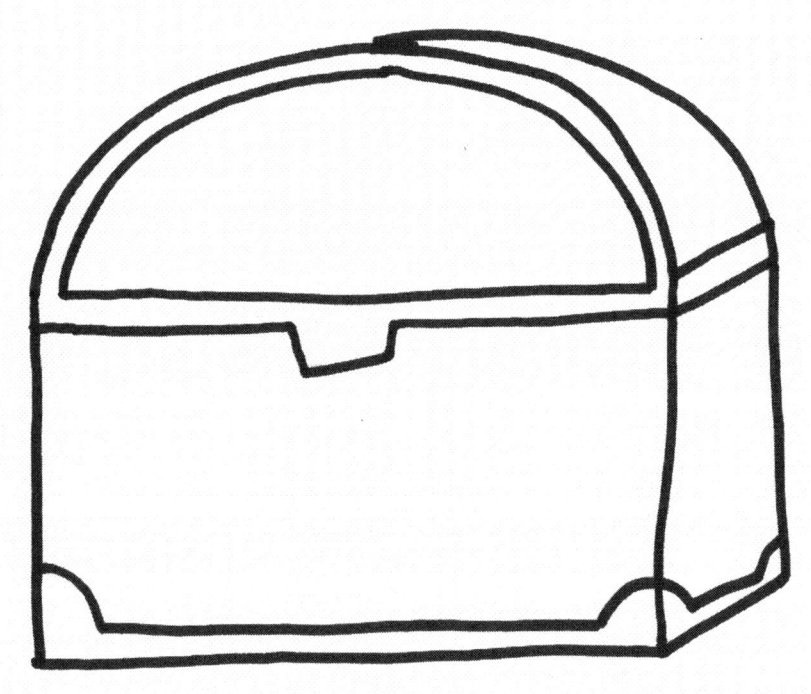

# Pat checks the chest.
# It is a sandwich and chips!

Pat and Max sip punch.
Pat and Max had a big lunch.

# The Skunk

By: Laura Nicholas

A skunk is in the hut.
The skunk is Pat's pal.

# Pat and the skunk drink milk.

The skunk spills his milk!
The skunk is sad.

Pat gets a rag.
Pat wets the rag at the sink.
Pat dabs the spill.

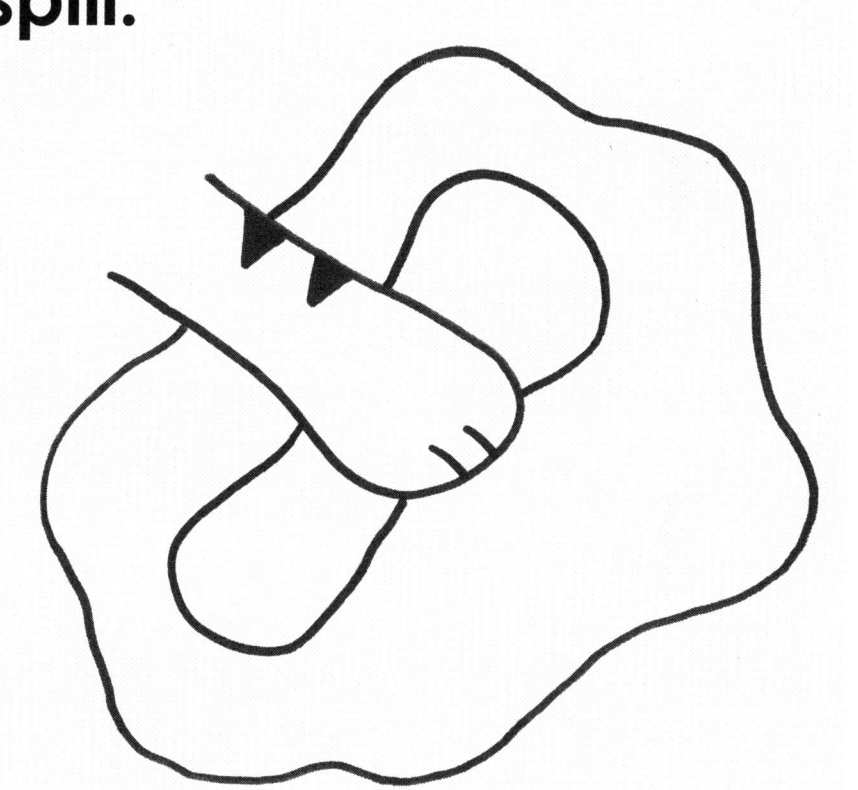

# The skunk is not sad.
# Pat is not sad.

# The Boat

By: Laura Nicholas

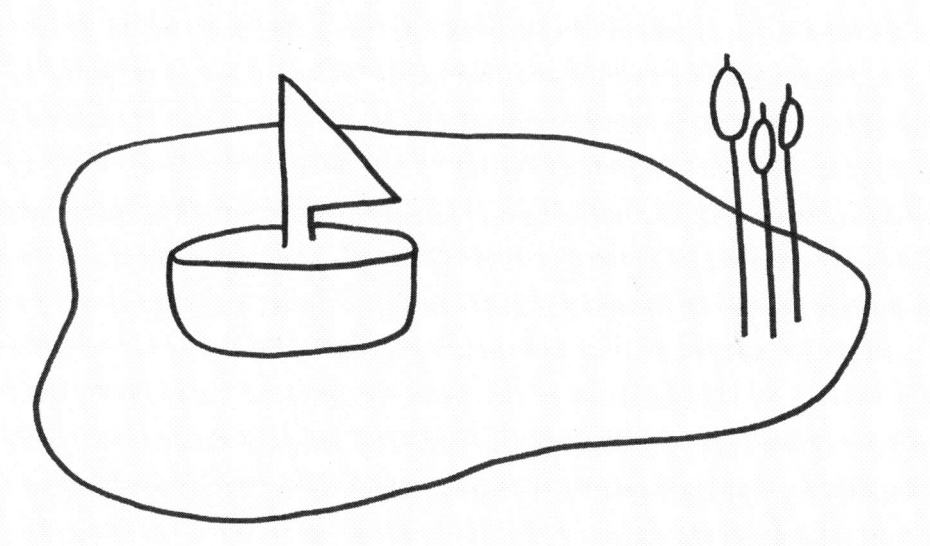

A boat is on the pond.
The boat floats.

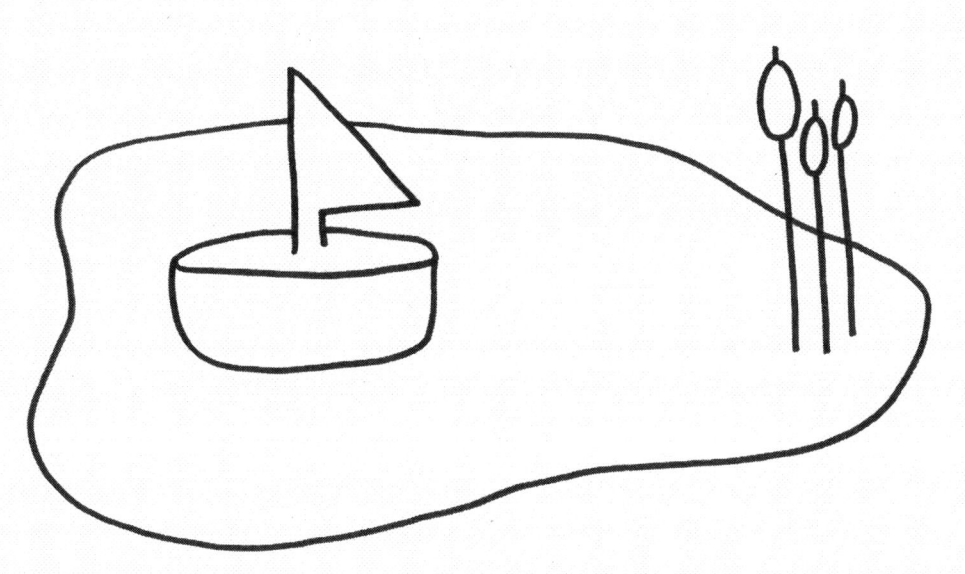

# A toad swims past the boat.

The boat rocks on the pond.
The boat still floats.

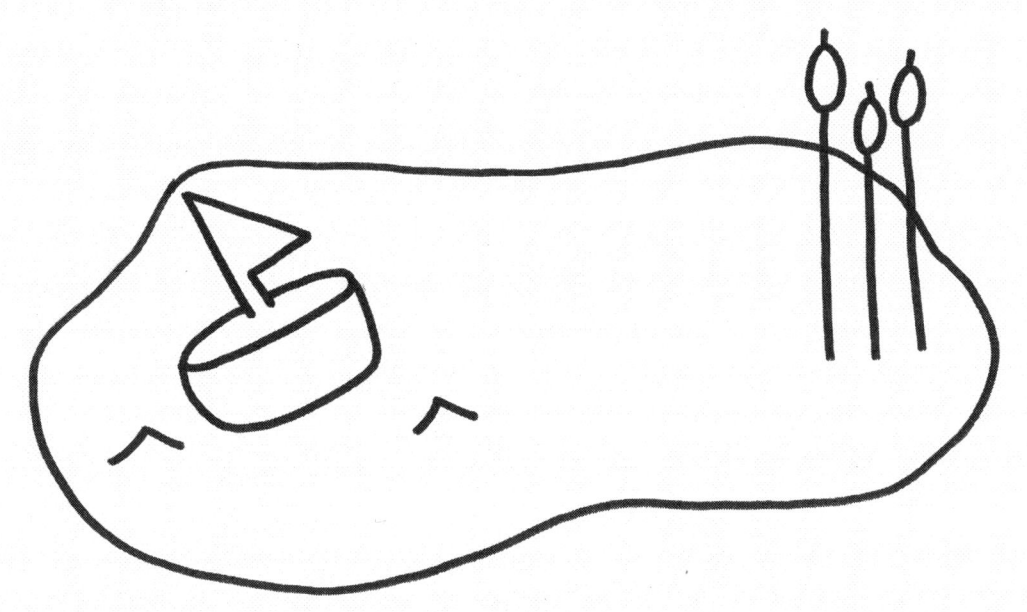

# A goat jumps in the pond.

# The goat soaks the boat.
# The wet boat still floats.

# The boat floats and floats.

# The boat is at the coast.

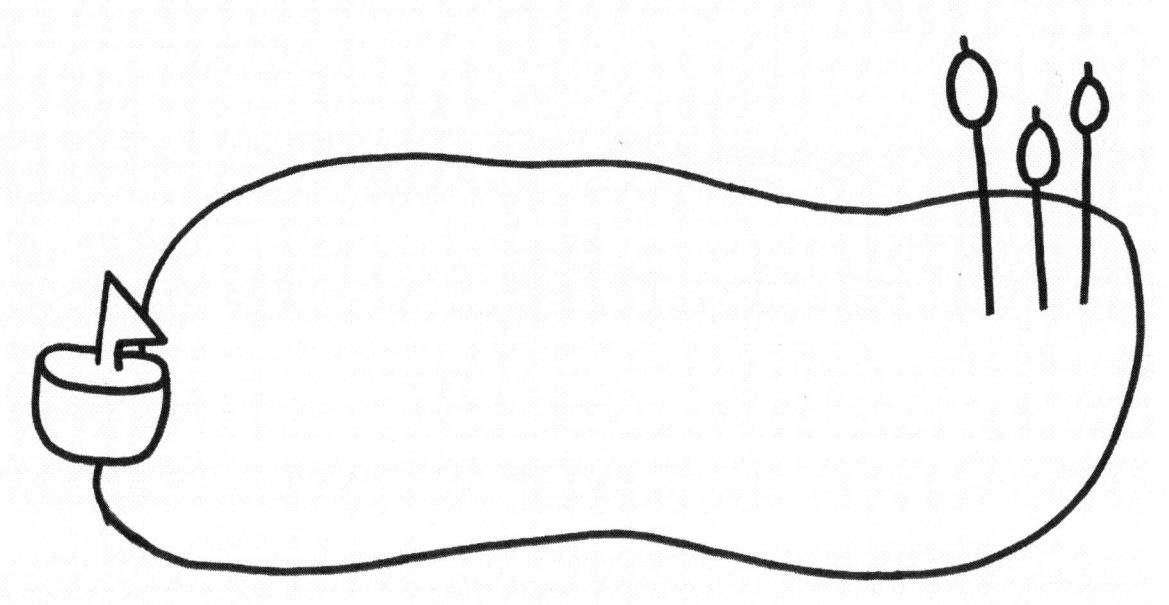

# The Beast

By: Laura Nicholas

Max cannot speak.
A beast is in the hut.
The beast is big.
It has a beak.

# The beast leaps.
# Max screams.

The beast is not mean.
It is just Pat.
Max is glad.

# Pat and Max sip tea and eat meat.

# The Cart

By: Laura Nicholas

# A cart is on the grass.
# Yarn is in the cart.

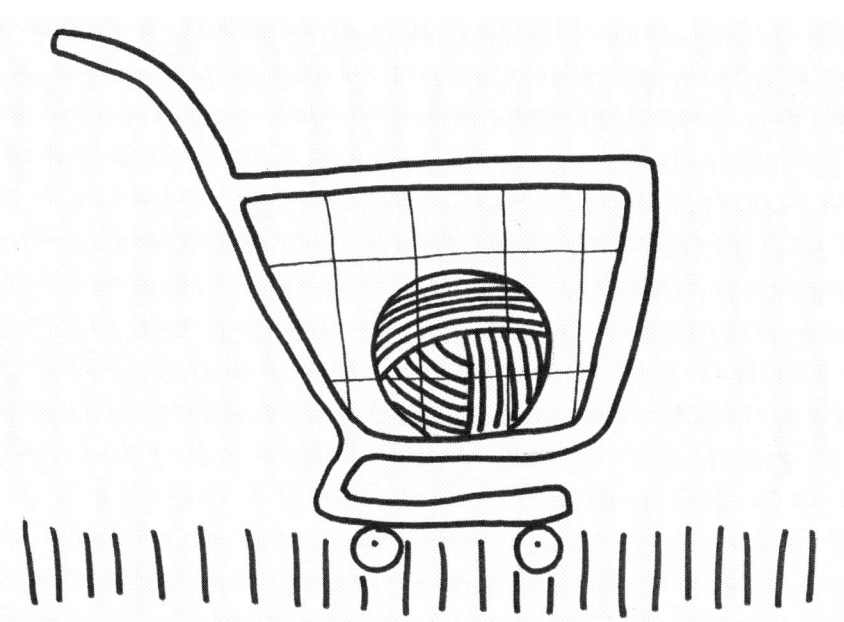

# The cart starts up the hill.

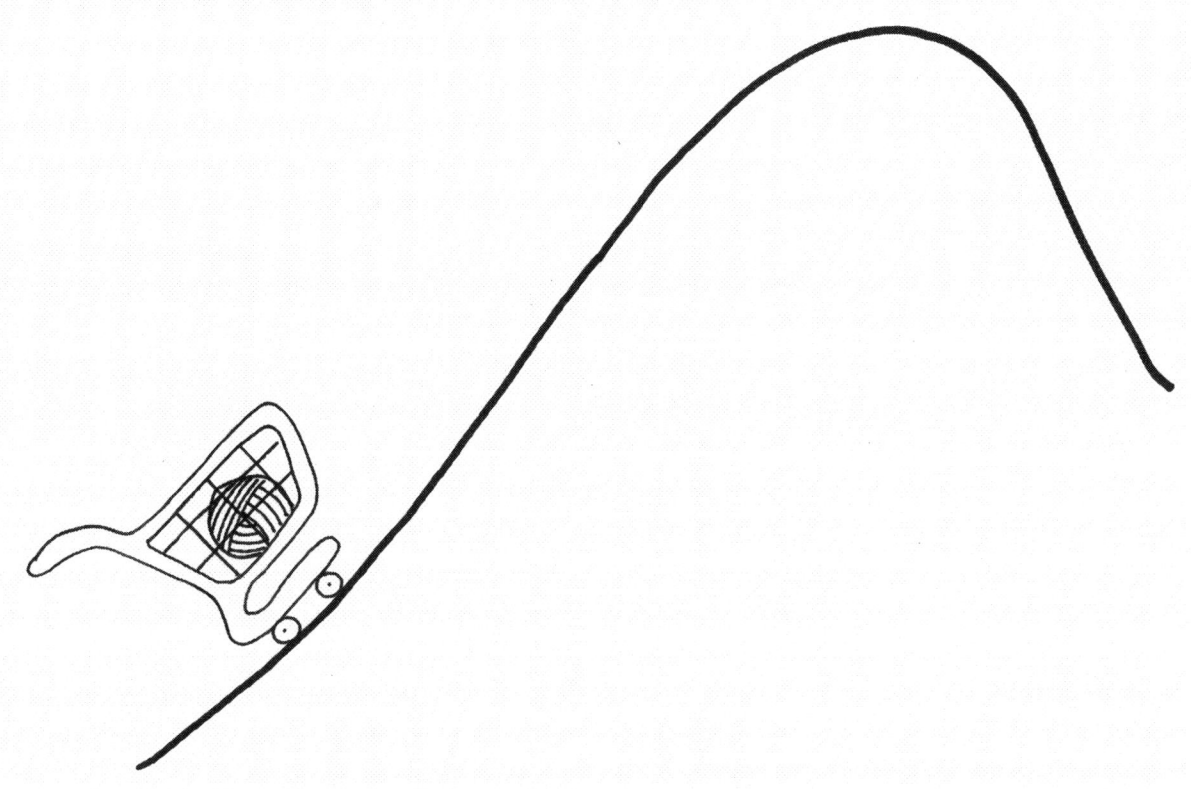

# The cart can get up the hill.

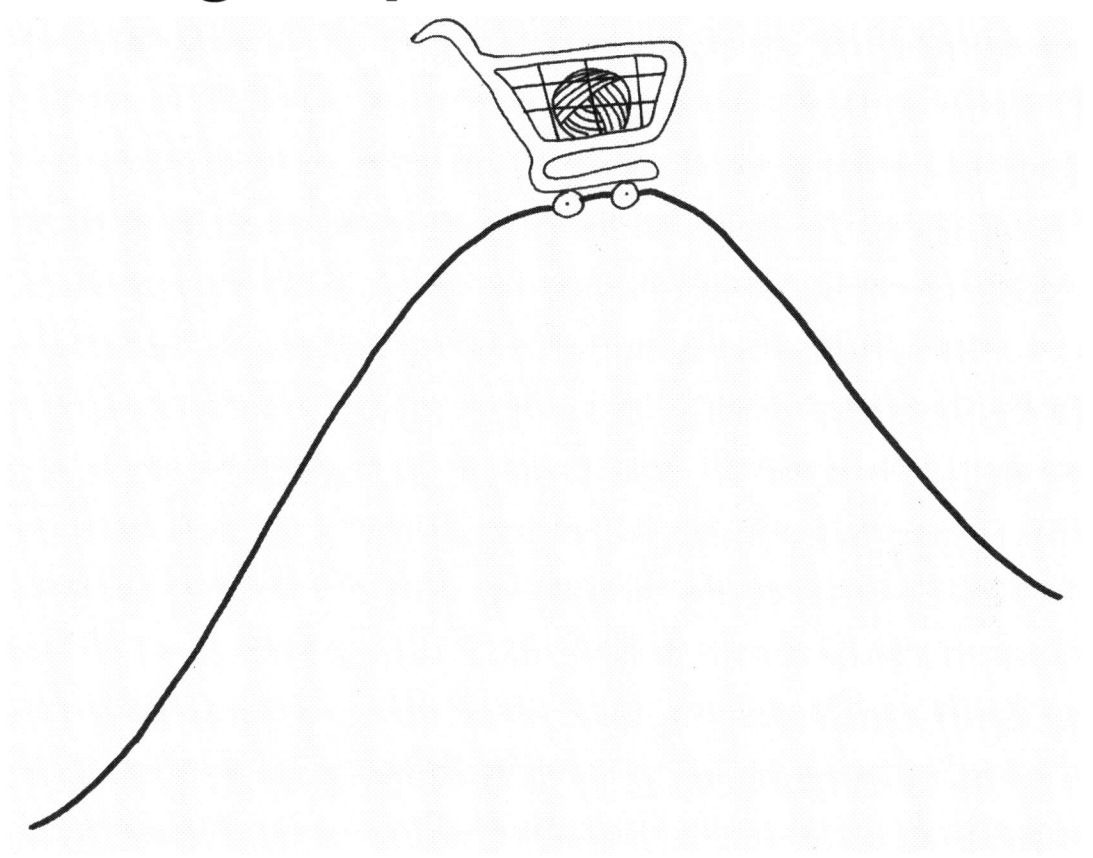

# A dog barks at the cart.

# The cart passes a farm.

The cart stops in the yard.
A cat can get the yarn.

The cat has fun.
The cat is glad.

# The Cloud

By: Laura Nicholas

The cloud is up.
The cloud is big.

**Droplets drip on the ground.
The grass gets wet.**

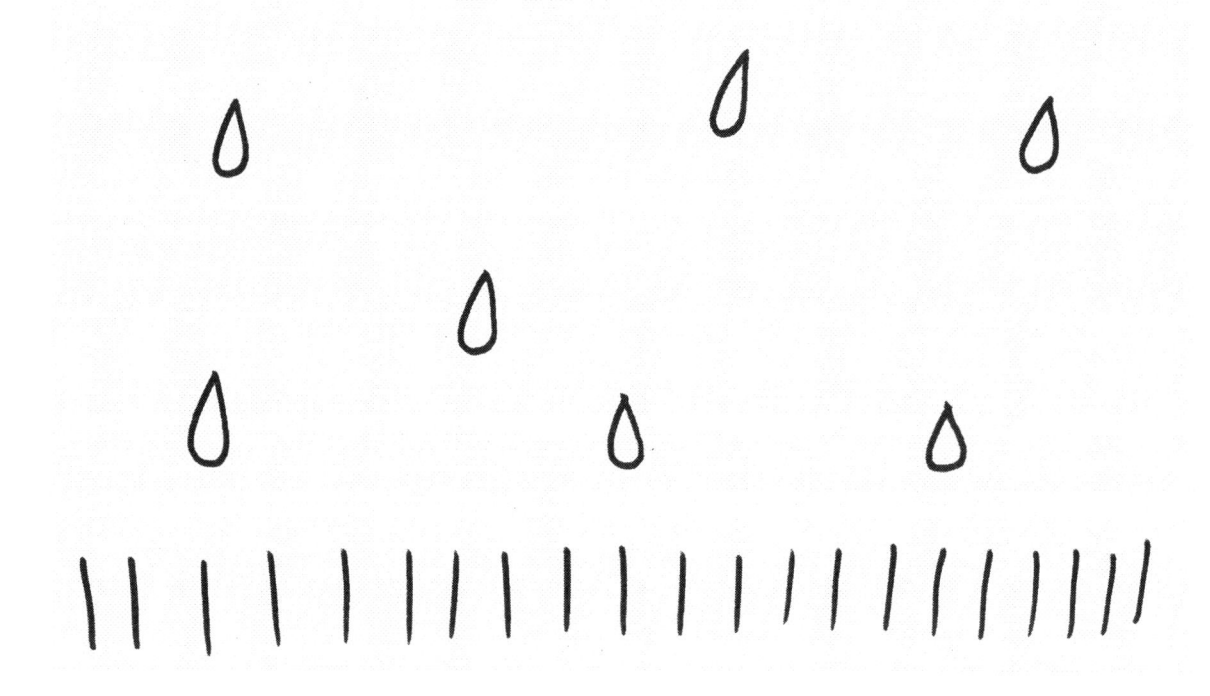

# A loud sound!
# Droplets pound on the ground.

# The droplets stop.
# The loud sounds stop.

# The cloud is not up.
# The sun is up.

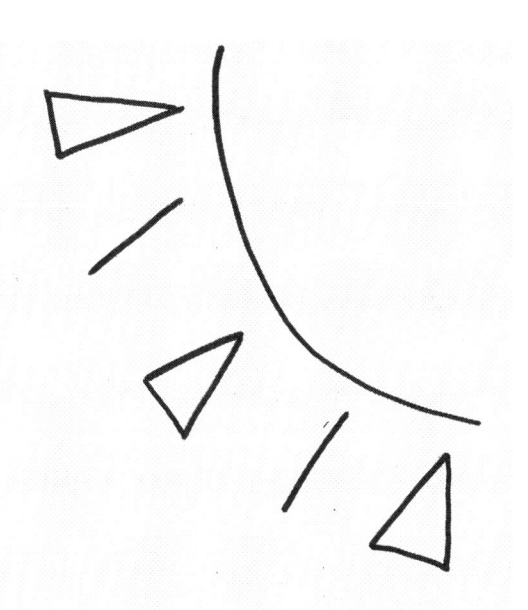

# The Cow

By: Laura Nicholas

A cow is in the pen.
The cow is brown.

# A sow jumps in the pen.
# The sow is the cow's pal.

# The sow and the cow snack on grass.

# The cow and the sow sit in the mud.

The cow and the sow had fun.
The sow jumps past the cow.

The cow is glad.
The cow naps in the pen.

# **The Bay**

By: Laura Nicholas

It is midday.
A crab is at the bay.
The sun is hot.

A stray dog trots up.
The crab snaps at the dog.
The dog runs away.

A ray swims up.
The crab snaps at the ray.
The ray swims away.

# The crab stays and plays.

# The Bird

By: Laura Nicholas

# A bird sits in a fir.

The bird flaps.
The bird gets up.

# The bird twirls and flips.

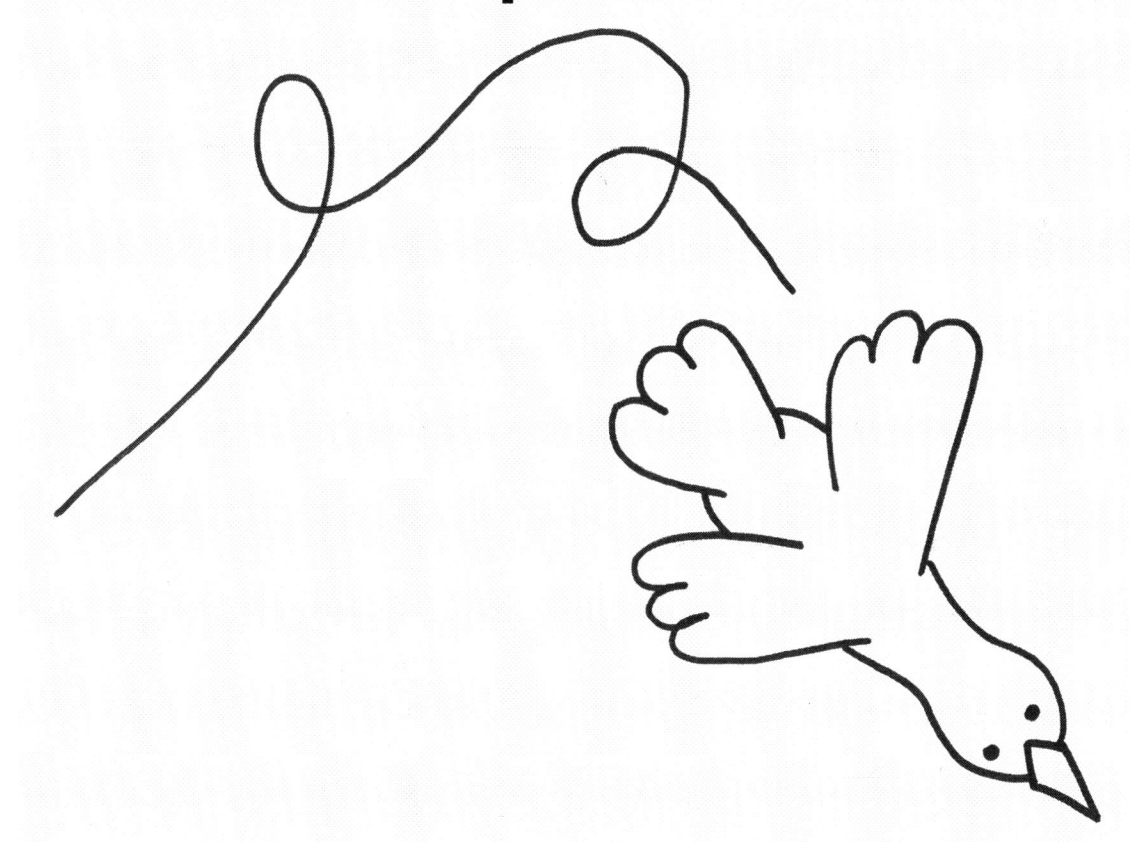

# The bird dips.
# The bird zips past the fir.

The bird lands on the fir.
The bird sits in the fir.
The bird rests.
The bird had fun.

# The Lawn

By: Laura Nicholas

It is dawn.
The sun is just up.
The lawn is in the sun.

# A cat crawls on the lawn.

The cat paws at the lawn.
The cat claws the lawn.

# The cat saw a bug on the lawn.

The cat yawns.
The cat sprawls on the lawn.
The cat naps on the lawn.

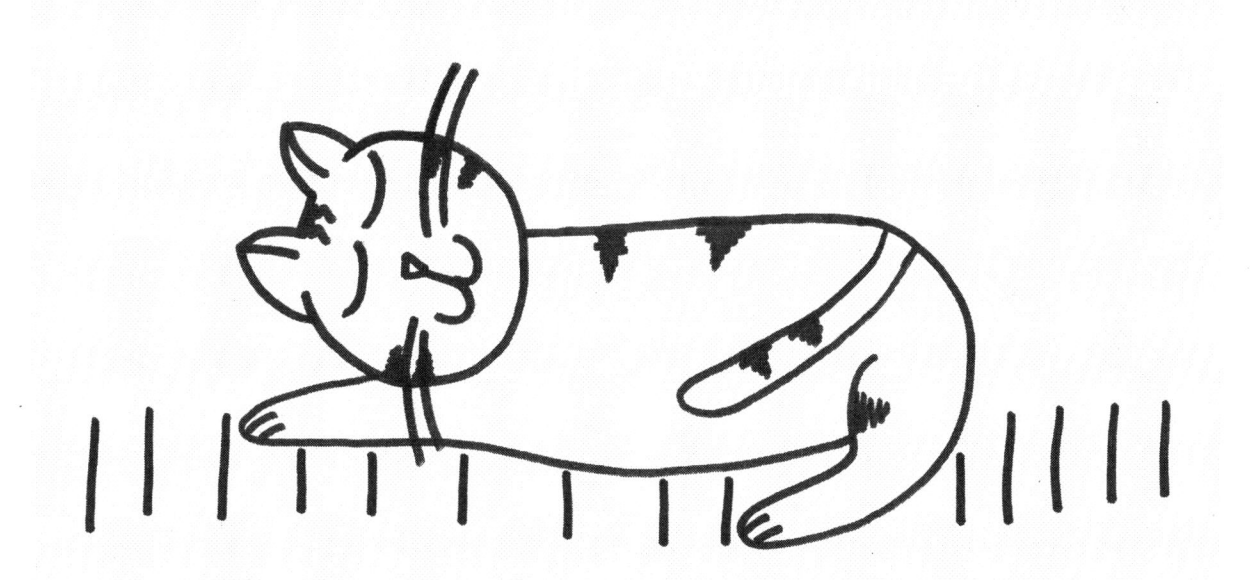

# The Fort

By: Laura Nicholas

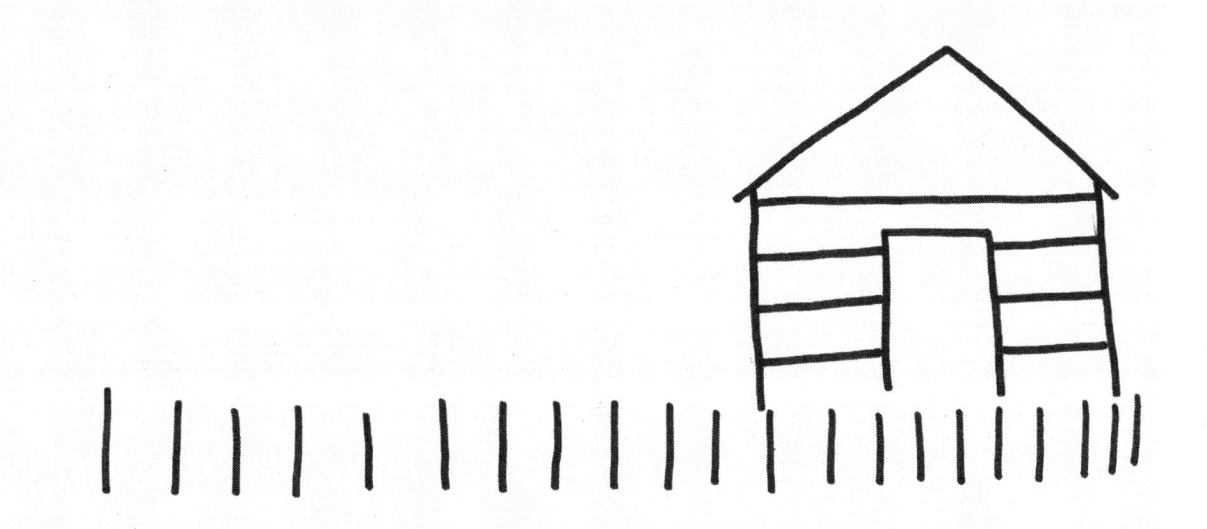

# Max has a fort.
# The fort is not big.
# The fort is on the grass.

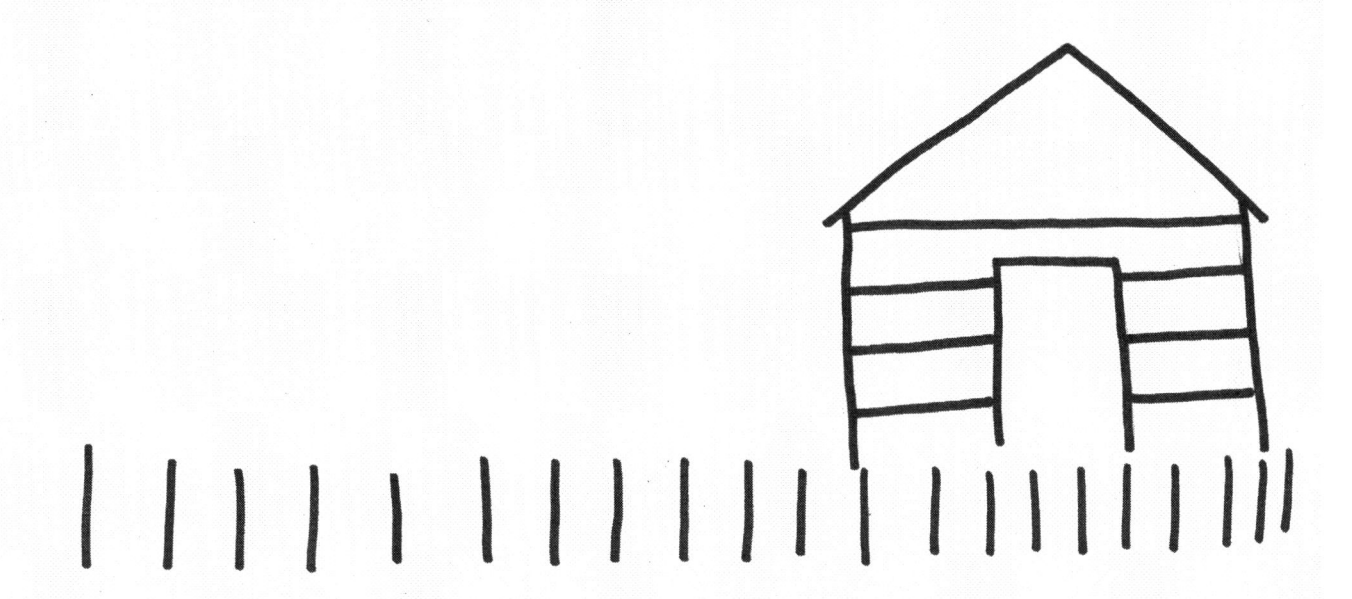

# Pat has corn for Max.
# Max lets Pat in the fort.

Max gets pork.
Pat and Max had corn and pork.

The sun is not up.
Pat and Max get in the hut.
Pat and Max had fun in the fort.

# The Spool

By: Laura Nicholas

Pat is in his room.
It is noon.
Pat has a spool.

Pat loops it.
Pat twists it.

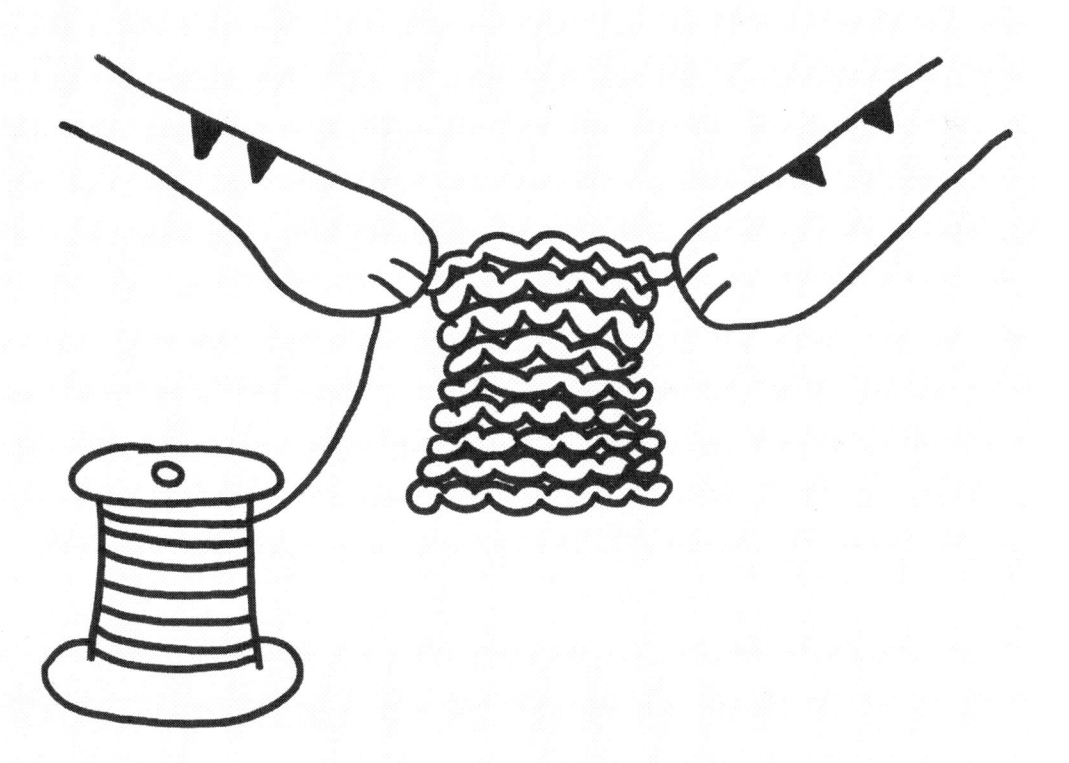

The moon is up.
It is cool.

Soon Pat has a hat.

Pat is not cool.
Pat can rest.

# The Eel

By: Laura Nicholas

# A weed is on the reef.
# The reef is deep.

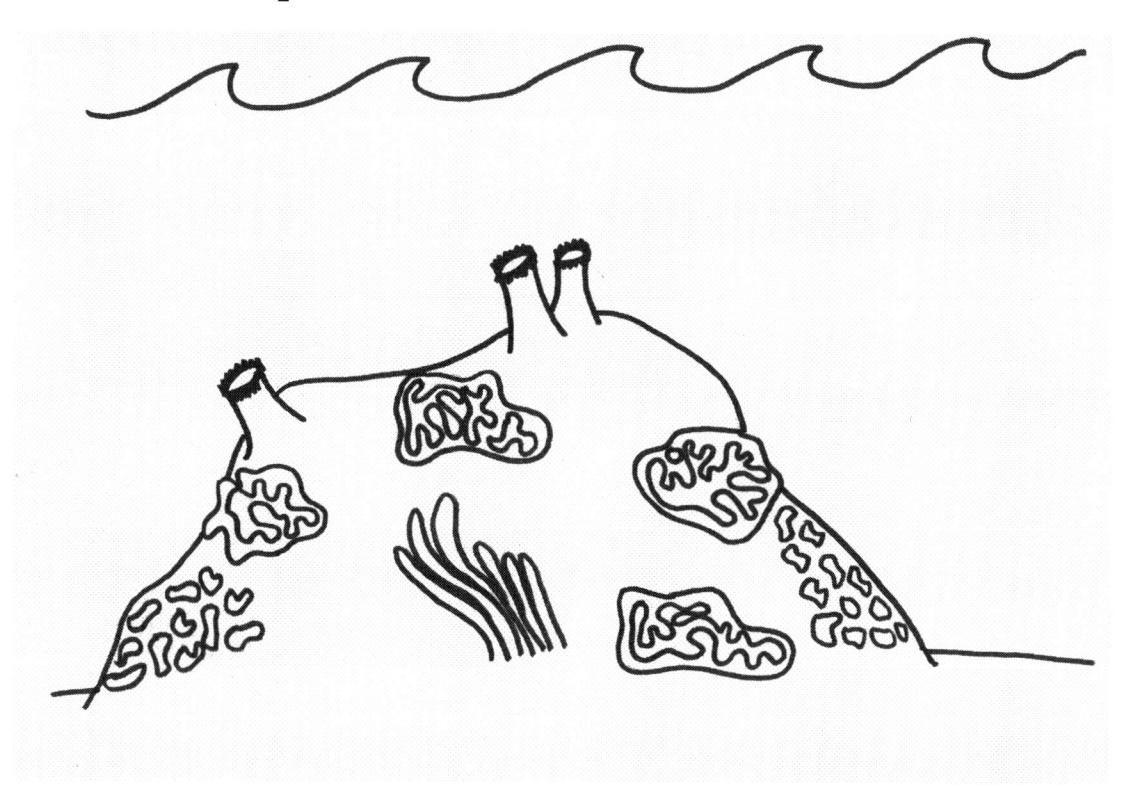

An eel swims past the reef.
The eel is deep.

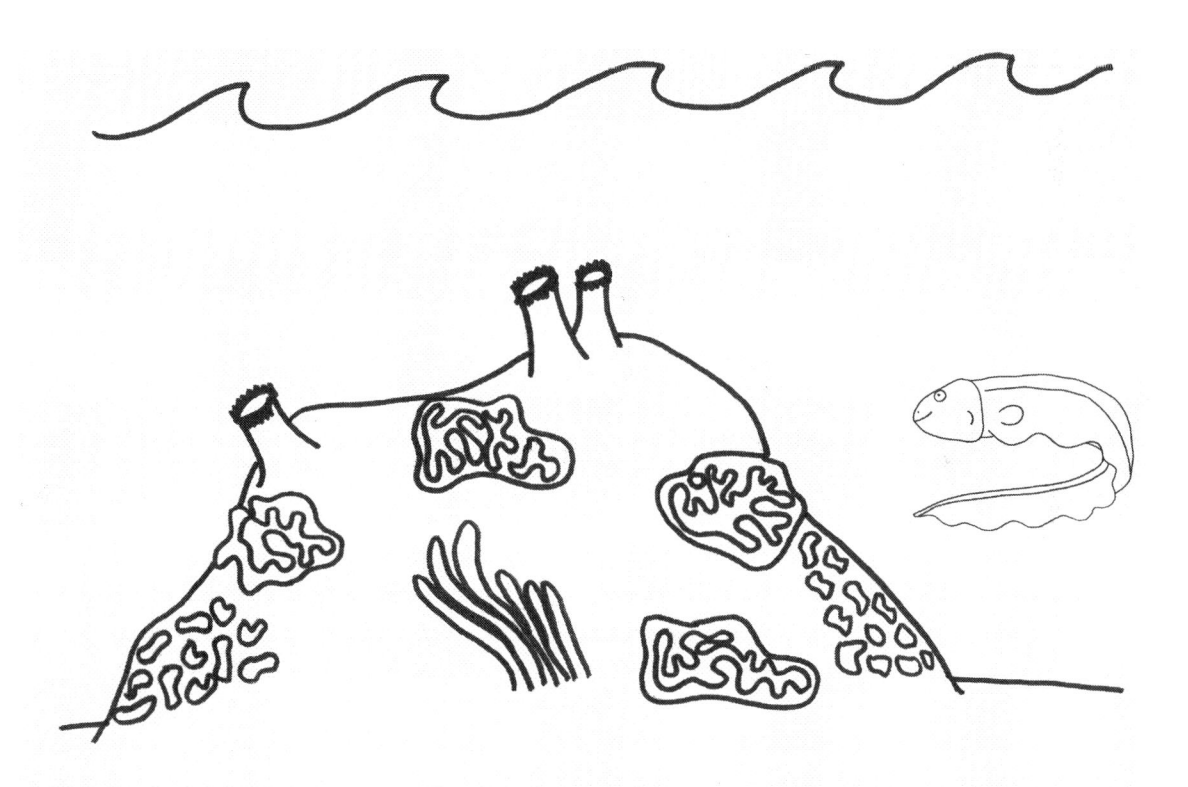

# The eel sees a crab stuck in the weed.

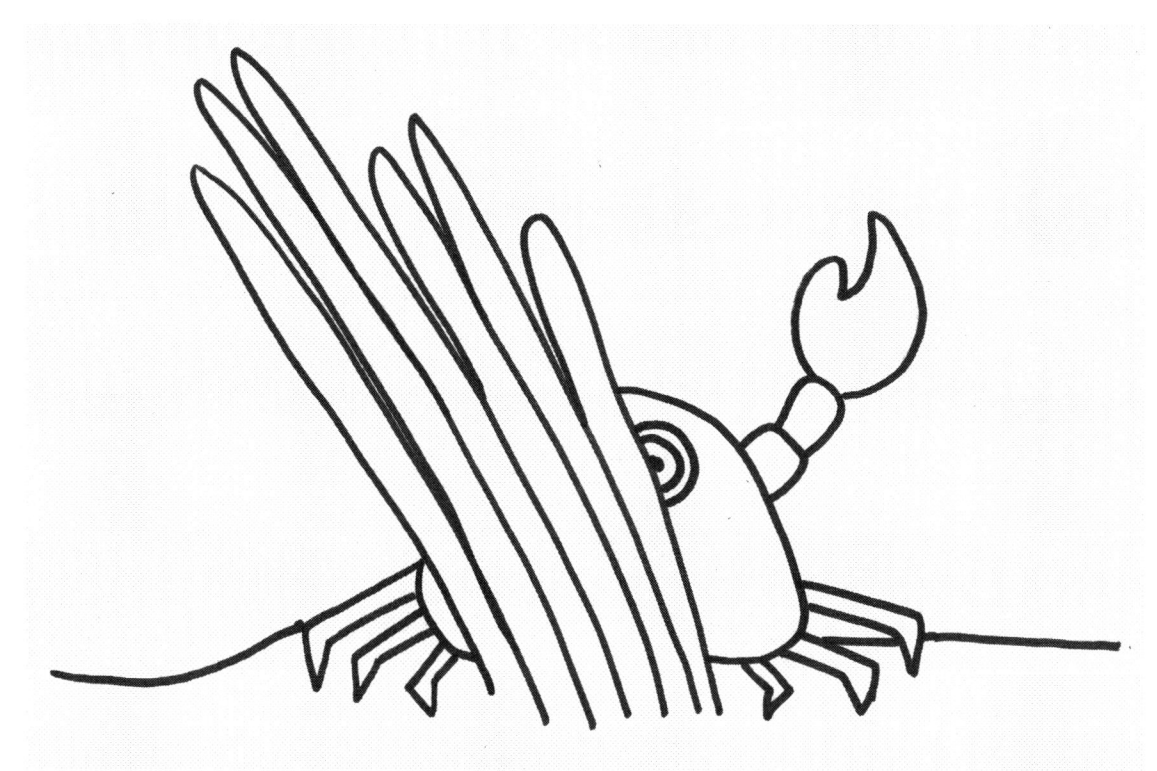

The eel frees the crab.
The crab creeps on the reef.

# The eel swims.

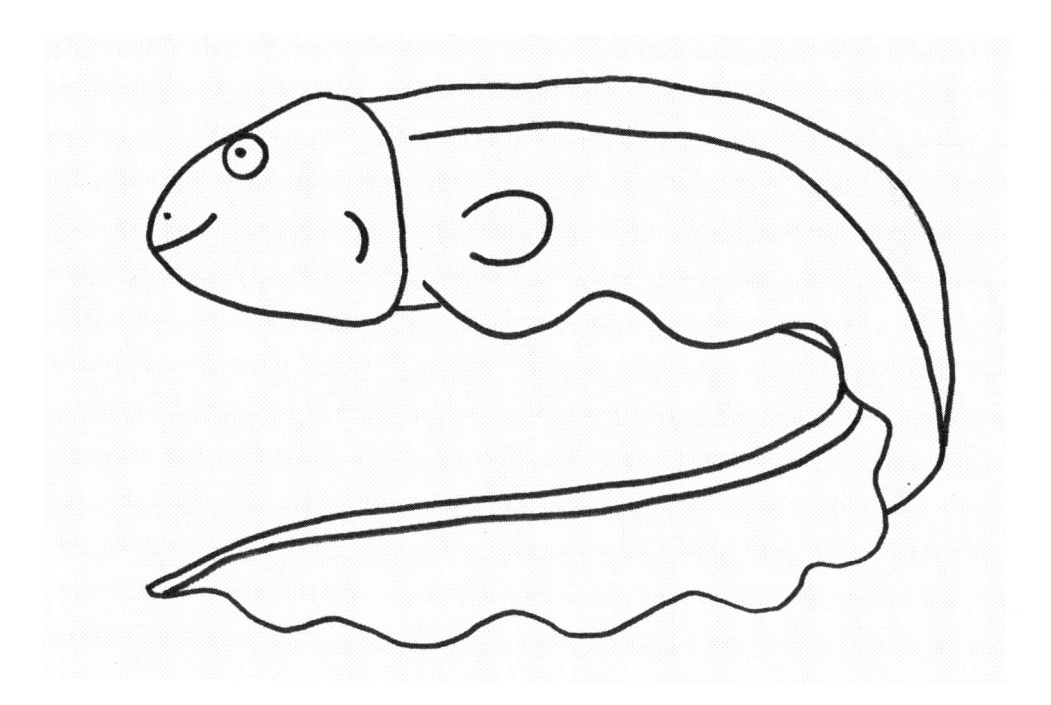

The eel stops and rests.
The eel sleeps.

# Quack!

By: Laura Nicholas

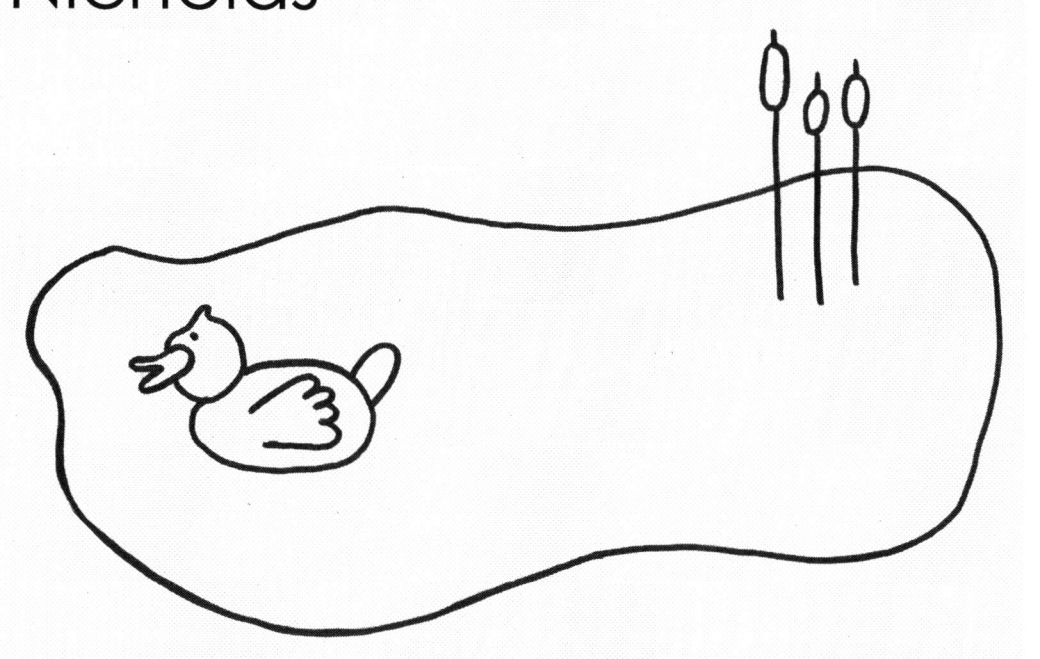

# A duck is on the pond.
# The duck quacks.

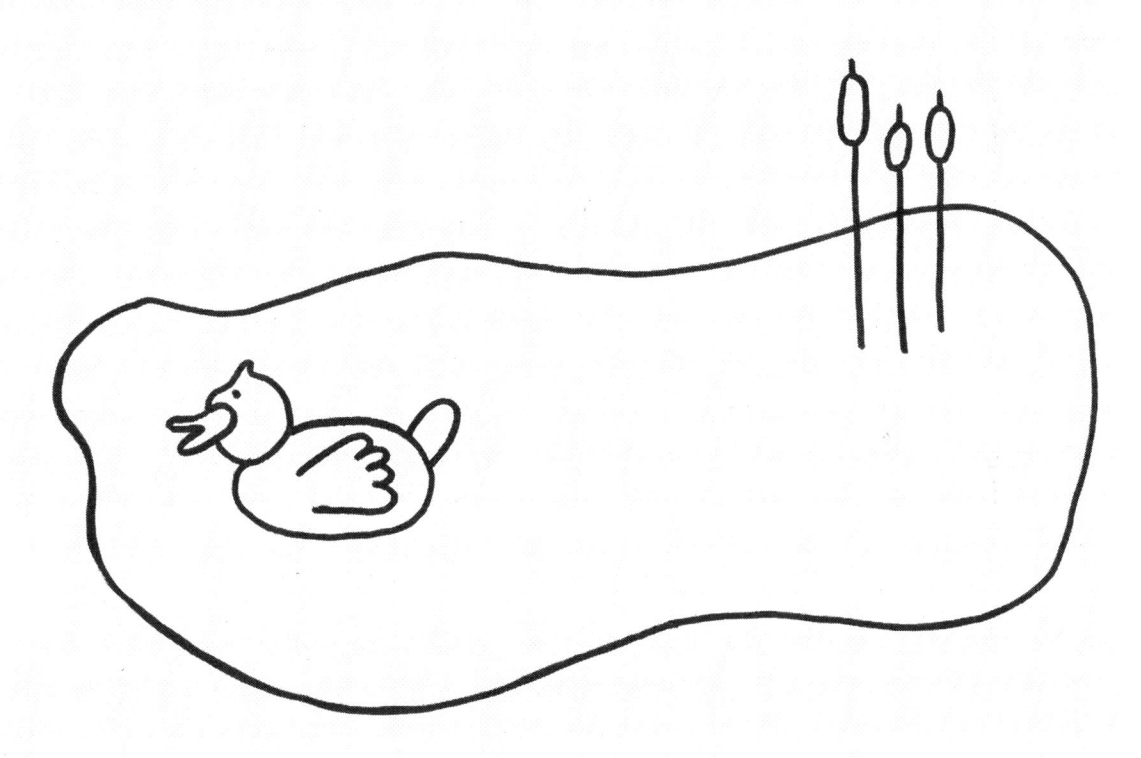

Ducks swim up.
The ducks quack.

The ducks quack.
Ducks swim up.
The quintet quacks as quick as it can.

The ducks quit.
The ducks swim off.
A duck rests on the pond.

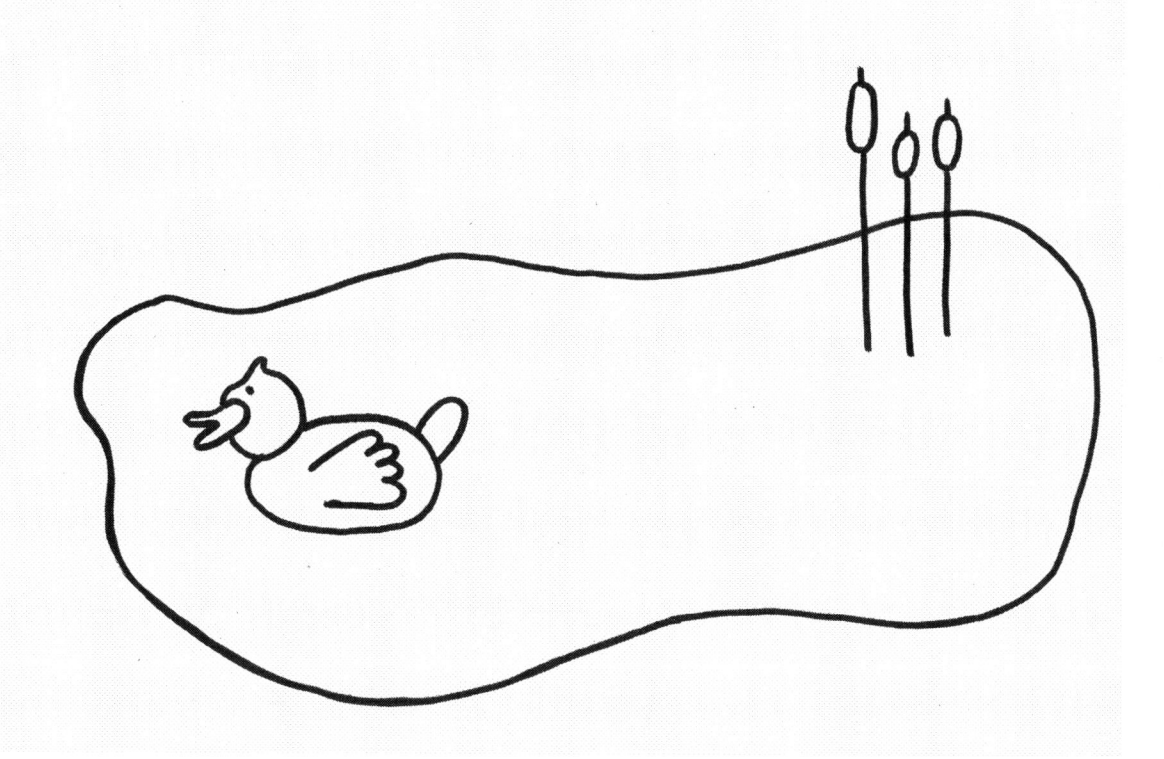

# The Bunny

By: Laura Nicholas

A bunny hops in the grass.
The bunny stops.

The bunny spots a puppy.
The puppy is happy.

The bunny and the puppy act silly.
The bunny and the puppy had fun.
The bunny has a pal.
The puppy has a pal.

The bunny is happy.
The bunny hops off and tells his mommy.

# **The Ball**

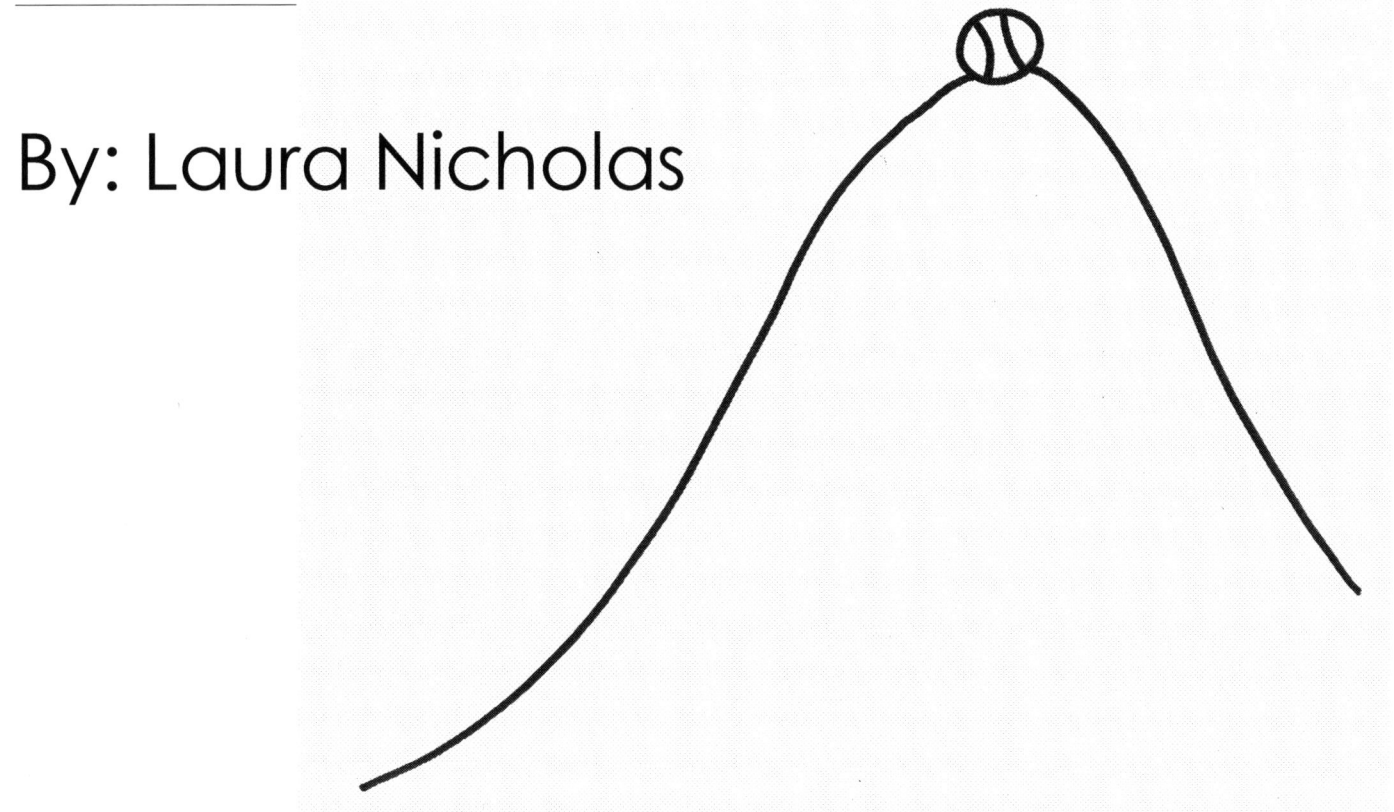

## By: Laura Nicholas

# A ball is on a hill.
# It is a small ball.

A cat bumps the ball.
The ball tips.
The ball falls.

# The ball hits a wall.

# A big dog nabs the ball.

The dog lets the ball fall.
The ball flips and flops.
The ball stops in the tall grass.

# The Cake

By: Laura Nicholas

# Pat bakes a cake.

# Pat frosts the cake.

# Pat cuts the cake.

# Pat sets the cake on a plate.

Max nips the cake.
Max is glad.

# Max gets a gift.
# Max rips the tape.

Max gets skates!
Max is glad.

# The Hole

By: Laura Nicholas

# A dog digs a hole.
# It is a big hole.

# The dog gets a bone.
# The bone is in the hole.

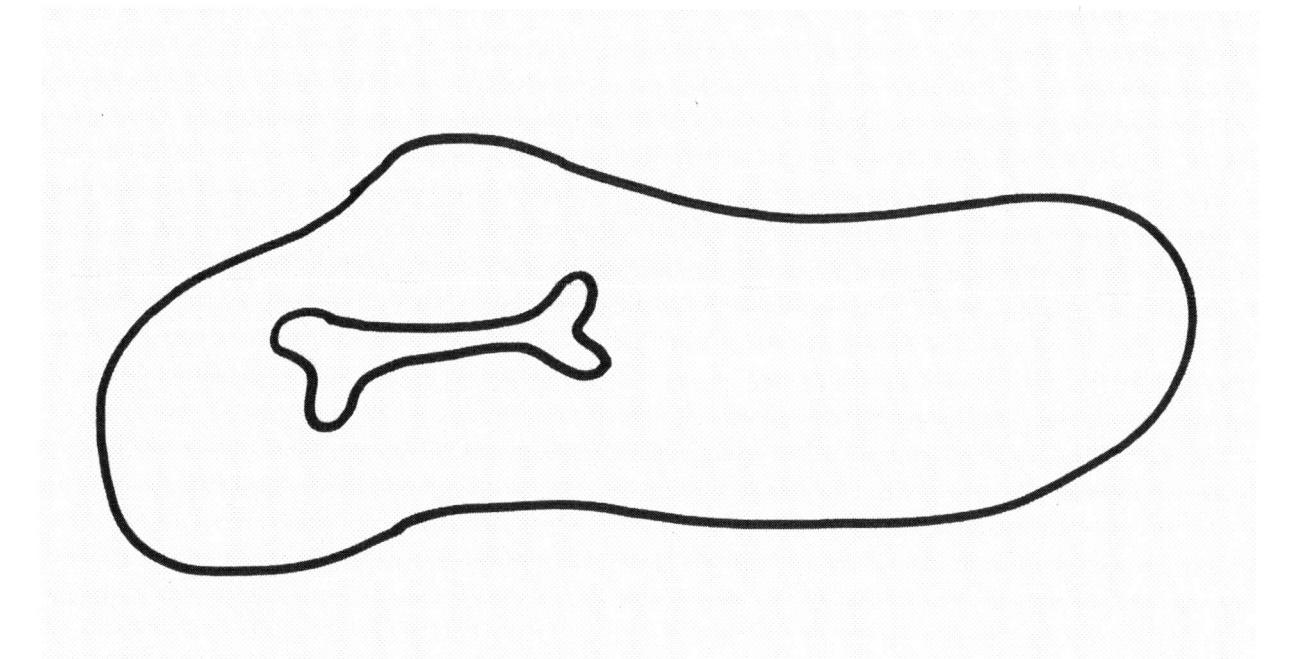

The dog gets a hose.
The hose is in the hole.

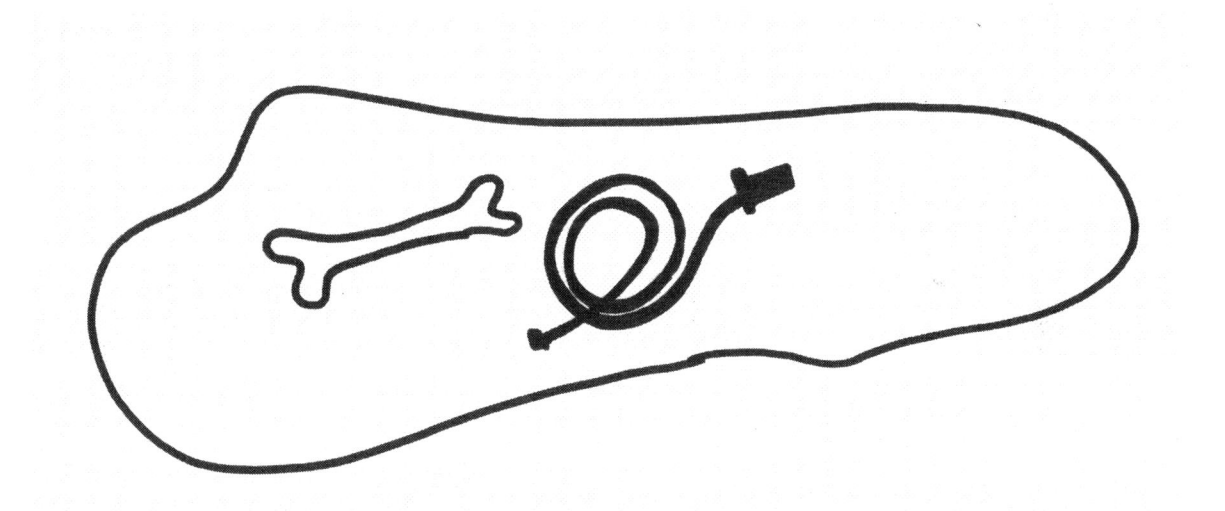

# The dog gets a globe.
# The globe is in the hole.

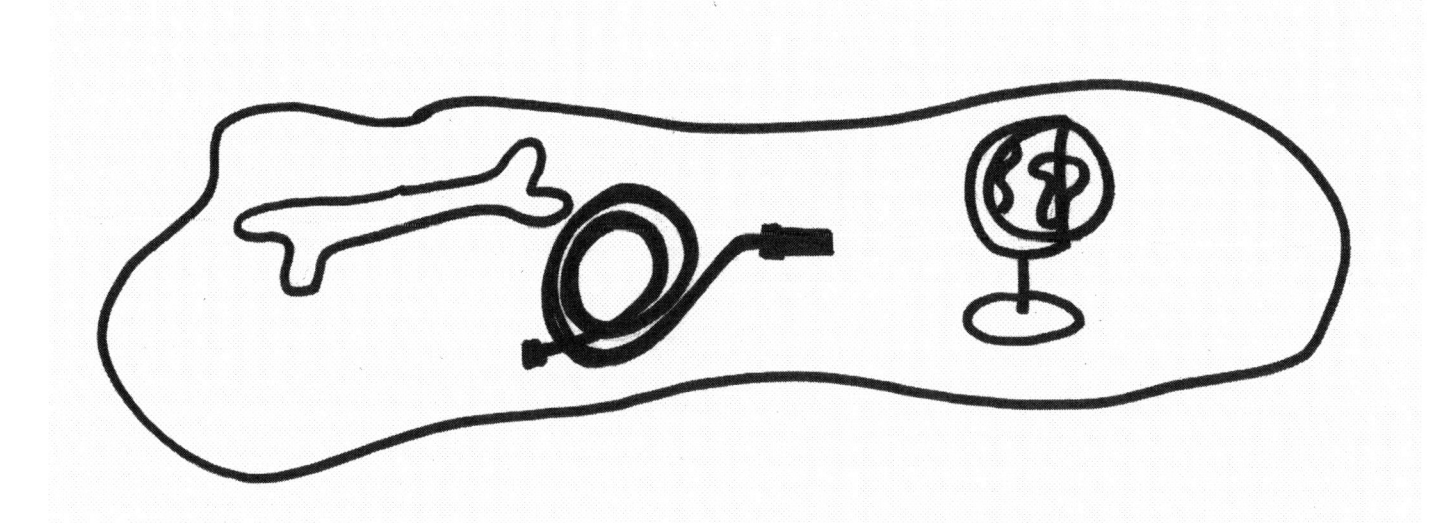

# The dog fills in the hole.
# The dog is glad.

# The Slide

By: Laura Nicholas

A slide is on the grass.
The slide has nine steps.
The slide has stripes.

# A cat jumps on the slide.

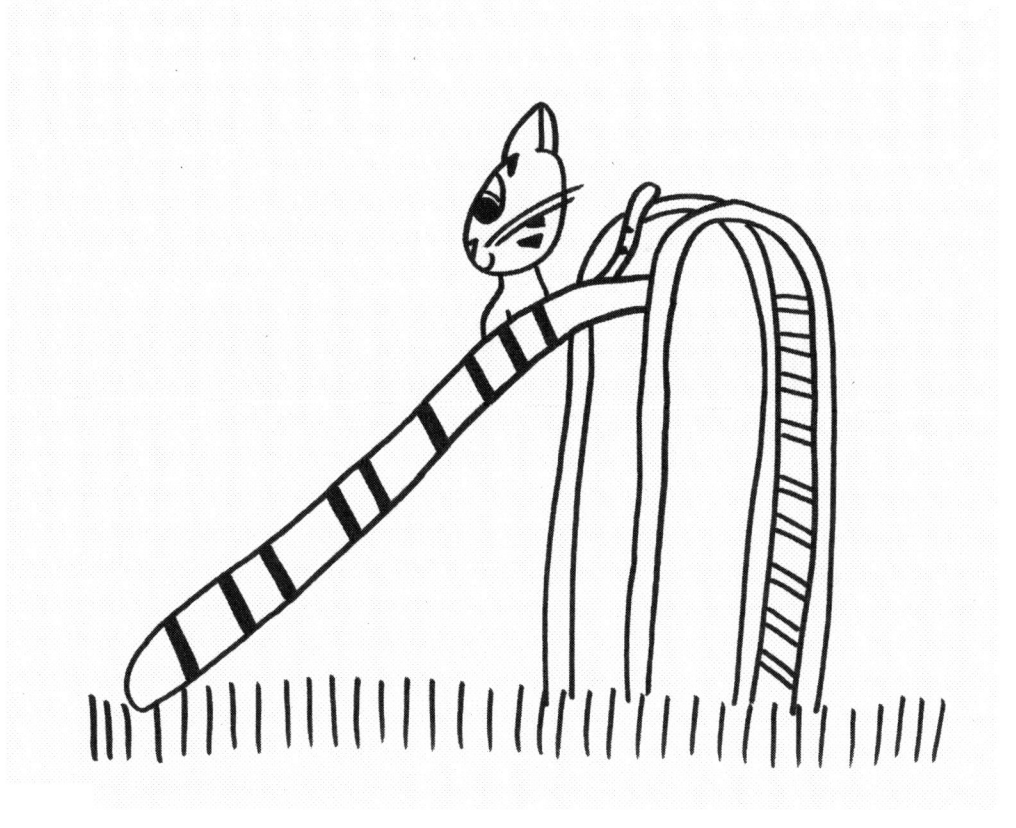

The cat slips on the slide.
The cat can smile.

# The cat jumps on the slide.

The cat slips on the slide.
The cat can smile.
The cat had fun.

# The Puzzle

By: Laura Nicholas

Pat has a puzzle.
The puzzle is on the mat.

It is not a simple puzzle.
Max can help Pat.

Is a kettle on the puzzle?
Is a bottle on the puzzle?
Is a candle on the puzzle?

# A pickle is on the puzzle!
# It is a pickle puzzle!

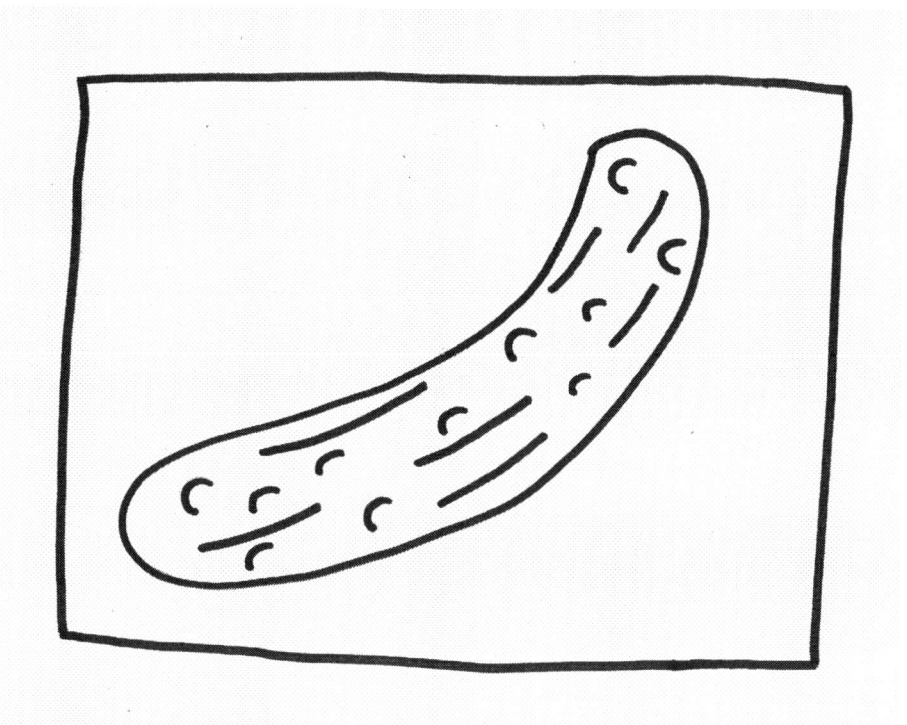

# Pat is glad.

# The Camel

By: Laura Nicholas

The camel is on the sand.
It is hot.

The camel passes a tunnel.
The camel did not stop.

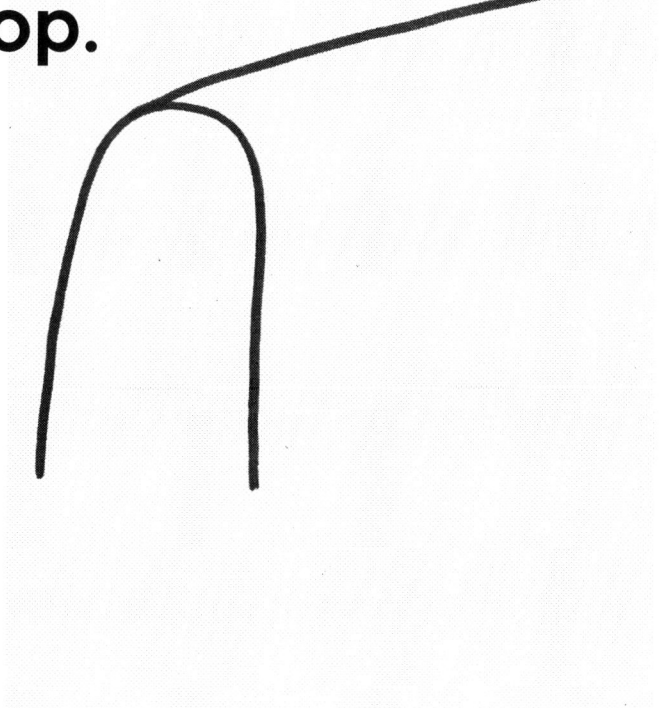

The camel passes a novel.
The camel did not stop.

# The camel is hot.
# The sun is hot.

The camel stops at a hostel.
The camel can rest.

# The String

By: Laura Nicholas

# A man is at the hut.
# The bell rings.

# Pat gets up.

The man brings a box.
String is in the box.

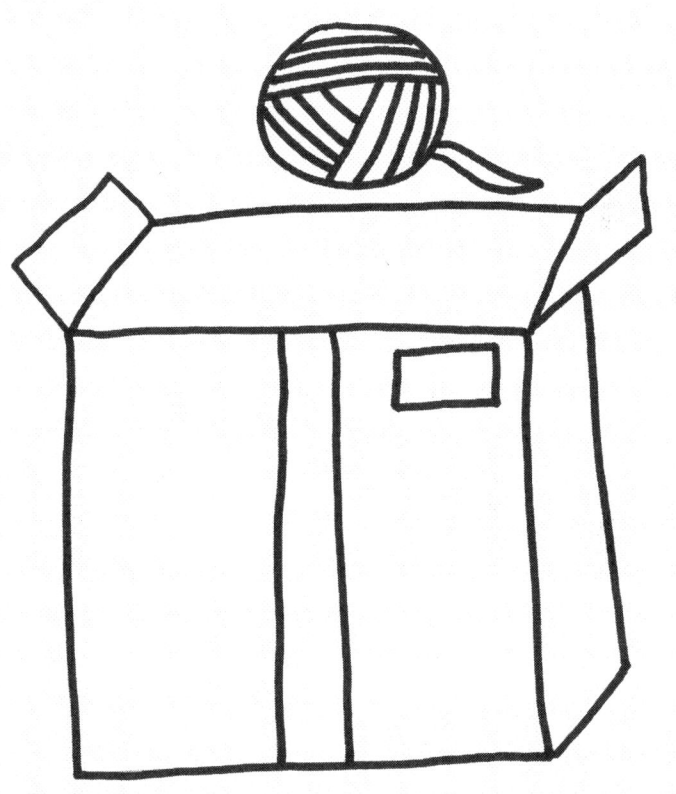

# Pat twists the string.

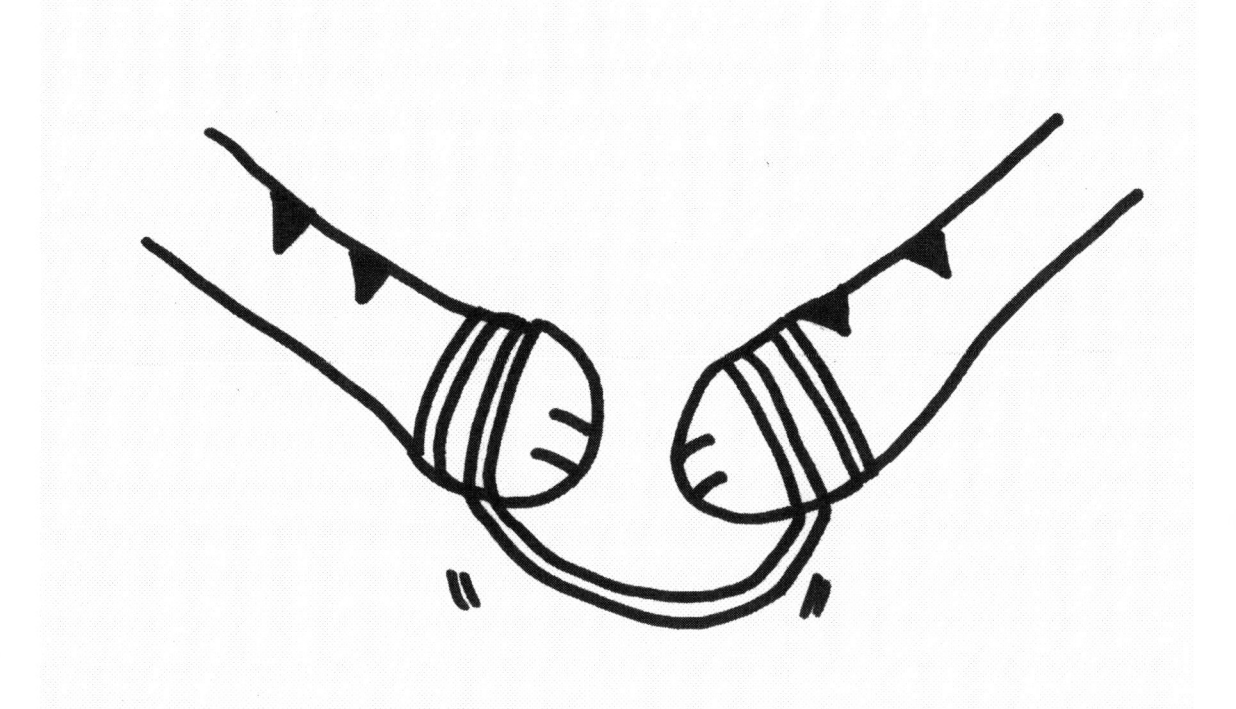

# Pat swings the string.

# Pat tosses the string up.

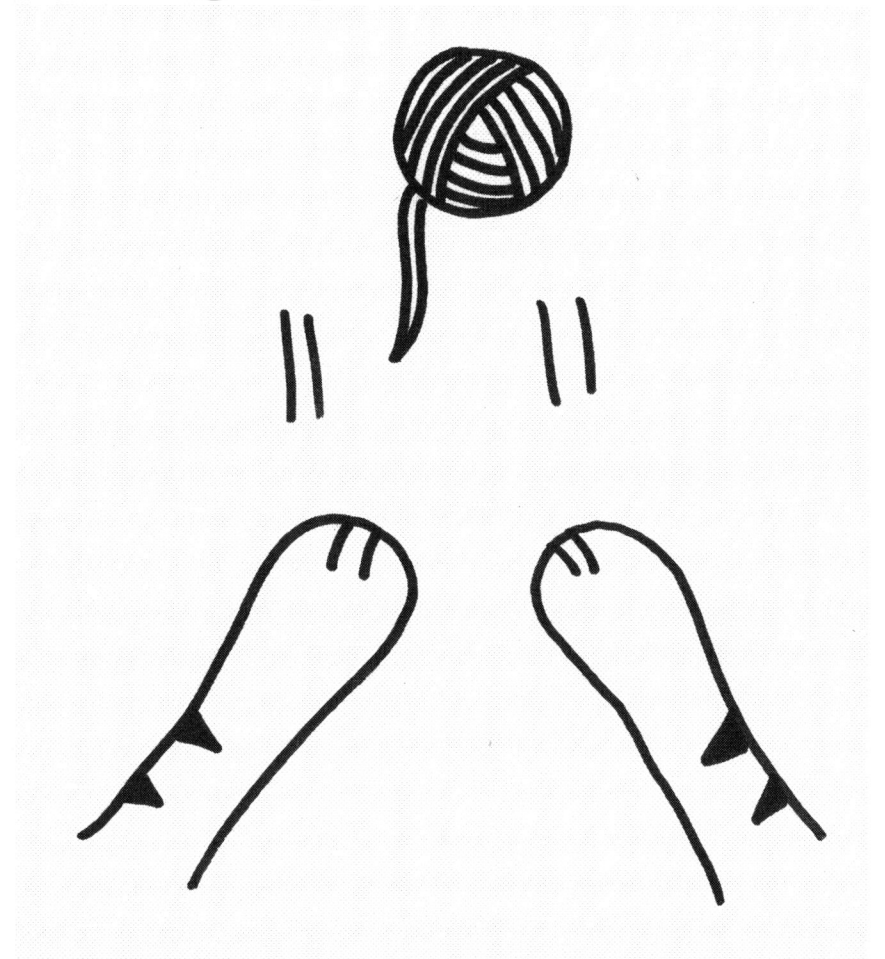

The string rips.
Pat is sad.

# The Light

By: Laura Nicholas

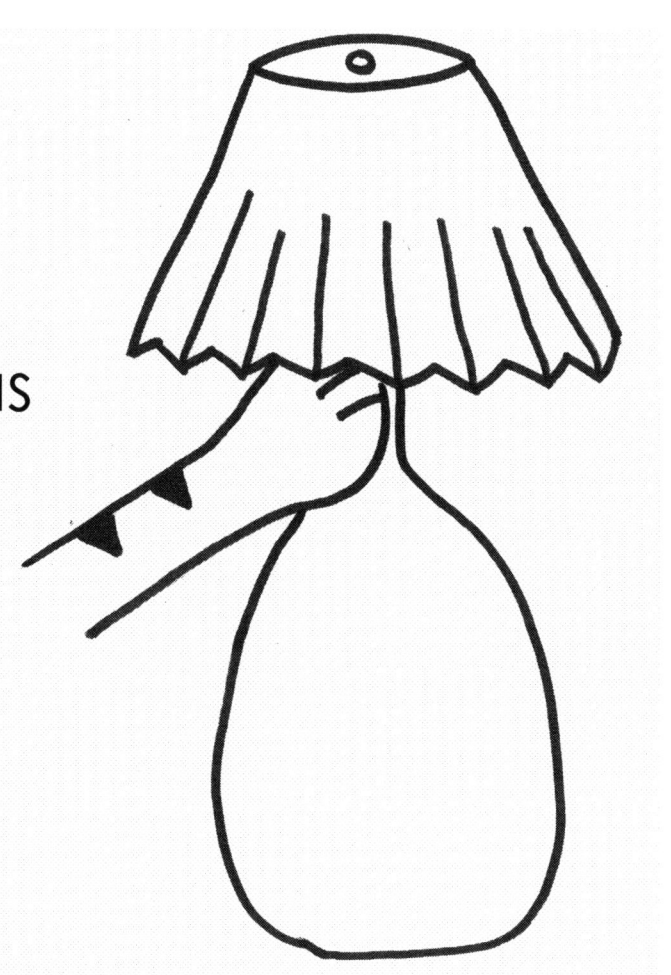

**It is night.**

The lamp is off.
The cat flicks on the light.

The lamp is bright.
The cat has sight.

# The cat gets a midnight snack.
# The cat has milk.

# The cat flicks off the light.

The cat gets in bed.
The cat rests until the sun is up.

Made in the USA
Middletown, DE
03 May 2020